SCREEN SMART SAM

Nicole Rawson

gatekeeper press™
Columbus, OH

Published by Gatekeeper Press

2167 Stringtown Rd, Suite 109

Columbus, OH 43123-2989

www.GatekeeperPress.com

Library of Congress Control Number: 2021936538

ISBN (hardcover): 9781662907302

ISBN (paperback): 9781662907319

eISBN: 9781662907326

Cover art by Emily Watson

Illustrations by Arnav Mazumdar

SCREEN SMART SAM!
BATTLES THE BAD HABIT MONSTERS

Welcome Parents!
Please visit www.ScreenSmartFamilies.org
to access special FREE resources to use with the book,
research links, and digital citizenship support materials.

This is Sam.

Sam loves to use all types of screens in elementary school and already has a smartphone.

Big screens, little screens, computer screens, phone screens.
Sam likes using all of them from a very early age.

Sam's bad habit monster pushes Sam to steal time for screens.

ALL - THE - TIME
on Sam's mind.

Sam loves to play video games and watch others play games. Sam likes to post pictures and look at pictures of other people. Sometimes Sam reads information on screens to help solve problems... but not often!

Early in the morning and late into the night, Sam spends lots of time on screens. Sam should be sleeping and growing. The blue light from screens is bad for eyes and sleep cycles, but the bad habit monsters keep Sam awake.

Sam and friends use their phones at the same time at lunch. But they only talk about what they see on screens. Sometimes kids get mean messages that cause sad feelings, but they don't even realize it's a problem.

The bad habit monsters keep screen time increasing and nobody notices.

Some pictures of classmates cause problems. Teachers tell their sweet students to keep phones at home, but Sam and friends love to sneak and use their phones at school.

Sometimes Sam sees bad pictures by accident, and doesn't say anything- but should! Sam just keeps on scrolling.

Sam uses screens to relax at home after school.
Mom is too tired to keep asking Sam to stop the screen time.
It makes her mad and sad.
But Sam doesn't care and doesn't stop.

Homework waits, or is
done in a hurry...
and often is

simply forgotten!

Dogs need walking, legs need stretching, weather needs watching... but the bad habit monsters keep screen time going. Sam plays on screens with friends - and chooses friends who have screens at home instead of playing outside.

Sam needs to reduce screen time, but it's so hard when a phone is constantly in hand. Planes land and cars drive by, but Sam doesn't even look out the window.

All thoughts point towards screens because that's what programs are designed to do - make kids obsessed!

In middle school, Sam plays sports...
but **extra time** is spent on screens.
Other teammates get better, but Sam stays the same.
On Sundays, Sam **sits all day** long looking at screens.

Sam thinks screens make people smart, but for kids,
too much screen time has serious consequences.
Sam knows smoking and drugs are bad, but games seem fun.
Sam is **grouchy** when there are no screens to see.
Sam's parents don't like Sam's new bad attitude.

Sam keeps feeling sad inside -- people in pictures are so pretty and seem so happy. Sam doesn't see all sides of the story and thinks life stinks. Even as an older teen, Sam's brain still doesn't always know when to stop using the apps designed to keep kids hooked. Bad habits keep growing.

Sam doesn't talk to classmates or try new things. Sam doesn't read books because screen time is always on the mind. Even when Sam watches movies, most of the time is spent staring at the phone.

Patience, gratitude, and humility can't be developed online. Sam gets older but the brain stays focused on screens. Sometimes Sam doesn't even attend school! Creativity is lost to cyberspace. Something needs to change – soon!

Finally, Sam's family decides screen time should **not** be **all the time.** Some new rules are set and all screens are taken away for a time. Sam is mad, but Sam's parents stand strong, knowing Sam's brain can't **self-regulate.**

The **new rules** help Sam stay on track. Sam's parents craft a media plan to guide the family. Screen smart kids of all ages need time for different activities to fully develop their brains and **emotions**. But it's not easy to fight the bad habit monsters!

New rules start to make sense. Sam signs a pledge to stay on the right path with the new routine. No screens in bedrooms, no screens in bathrooms. No screens in cars, no phones at the dinner table or while watching TV. Family time comes first!

A cool new phone just for kids keeps Sam safe and distraction free, making it easy to limit time and stay busy offline. Sometimes, Sam thinks this isn't fair, but the new routine stays in place. Sam starts to enjoy not worrying about what apps to check next, keeping the bad habit monsters away.

Screens are turned off at the same time every night and parked in a box to build healthy habits. New screen rules sometimes seem impossible, but Sam is adjusting and screen smart parents stand strong.

Without so much screen time, Sam is bored. Without screens, Sam sleeps. Sam is growing and needs a lot of sleep to stay healthy. Sam sometimes can't think about what to do without screens, but feels better with the new routine!

Sam starts to enjoy walks. Walks with the dog and walks to shops. Sam keeps feeling better and starts to smile more. Without the bad habit monsters, Sam talks about different subjects and thinks about new activities.

Even Sam's younger sister has a different screen routine than others, keeping playtime screen-free. Sam's parents are careful to set up monitoring systems and controls to help keep the whole family safe online all the time. It's never too young to be screen smart!

Sam starts to read more books. Without distractions, there is more time to do homework and even help others. Sam's teen brain can focus more easily and grades improve without the wasted free time on screens!

The. **thoughts of screens** always stay, but Sam becomes happy and healthy. Sam's parents help keep the new routine, and keep the kids **on track** even though screens are created by machines to keep people coming back.

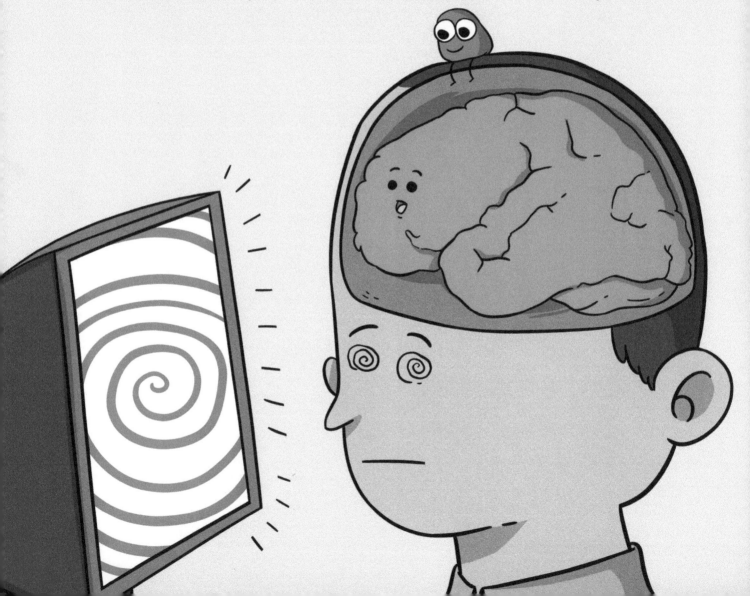

Sam learns to use screens responsibly. Sam sets screens aside, uses computers as a tool, and chooses to spend time with people over time online. Sam thinks about the future and is careful to keep screen time limited.

Sam's new way of interacting
with screens as a teen
creates healthy digital habits for life!

Sam's sister is happy to grow up
without constant tech temptations.

Sam's parent's feel confident about
guiding with healthy boundaries,
even when it wasn't always easy.

Sam's family is proud
to be screen smart!

CPSIA information can be obtained
at www.ICGtesting.com
Printed in the USA
LVHW070626040621
689326LV00002B/7